31472400221432

P9-CIU-034

# THE UNITED STATES OF
# MURDER INC.

# TRUTH

# THE UNITED STATES OF MURDER INC.

# TRUTH

Created by
## BRIAN MICHAEL BENDIS
## & MICHAEL AVON OEMING

Colors: TAKI SOMA

Letters: CHRIS ELIOPOULOS

Editing & Production: JENNIFER GRÜNWALD

Business Affairs: ALISA BENDIS

Collection Designer: PATRICK MCGRATH

**THE UNITED STATES OF MURDER INC. VOL. 1: TRUTH**. Contains material originally published in magazine form as THE UNITED STATES OF MURDER INC. #1-6. First printing 2015. ISBN# 978-0-7851-9150-6. Published by MARVEL WORLDWIDE, INC., a subsidiary of MARVEL ENTERTAINMENT, LLC. OFFICE OF PUBLICATION: 135 West 50th Street, New York, NY 10020. Copyright © 2014 and 2015 Jinxworld, Inc. All rights reserved. Powers, its logo design, and all characters featured in or on this issue and the distinctive names and likenesses thereof, and all related indicia are trademarks of Jinxworld, Inc. ICON and its logos are TM & © Marvel Characters, Inc. No similarity between any of the names, characters, persons, and/or institutions in this magazine with those of any living or dead person or institution is intended, and any such similarity that may exist is purely coincidental. $24.99 per copy in the U.S. and $27.99 in Canada (GST #R127032852); Canadian Agreement #40668537. **Printed in the U.S.A.** Manufactured between 1/19/2015 and 3/2/2015 by R.R. DONNELLEY, INC., SALEM, VA, USA.

10 9 8 7 6 5 4 3 2 1

IN MY DAY, THIS CEREMONY WENT A LITTLE DIFFERENTLY.

IT WAS DONE IN A BACKROOM. AWAY FROM THE WORLD.

AND YOU HAD TO EARN IT WITH A LIFETIME OF SERVICE.

YOU HAD TO BE MORE THAN JUST BLOOD.

YOU HAD TO PROVE YOUR WORTH AND LOYALTY.

BUT YOUR FATHER, AND HIS FATHER BEFORE HIM... THEY WERE TRULY HONORABLE MEN.

IN MANY WAYS THEY WERE THE BACKBONE OF THIS ORGANIZATION, THIS FAMILY...

I WOULD MAKE AN EXCEPTION FOR YOU, VALENTINE, EVEN IF OUR WAYS HAD NEVER CHANGED.

TAKE THE KNIFE.

WHO WE ARE IS WHO YOU ARE.

DO YOU AGREE?

YES, SIR.

SHOW US.

ALL RIGHT.

YOU CAN THANK HIM FOR THAT TOO.

HE'S WAITING FOR YOU.

VALENTINE.

MR. TUZZO.

SO, YOU READY TO GET DOWN TO IT?

'COURSE.

YOU UNDERSTAND YOU WON'T BE WORKING THE POKER GAMES IN TOWN ANYMORE.

I ACTUALLY *DIDN'T* KNOW THAT.

YOU'RE A MADE GUY NOW.

YOU DON'T NEED TO BE WIPIN' COLLEGE SHITHEADS' ASSES ANYMORE.

YOU'RE EVENTUALLY GONNA HAVE PEOPLE DOIN' THAT FOR YOU.

SO, UH, WHAT *WILL* I BE DOING?

TELL HIM.

TODAY YOU'RE GOING ON A LITTLE TRIP. AS A REPRESENTATIVE OF *OURS*.

OH.

YOU'RE GONNA GO TO D.C. AND DELIVER THIS TO A GUY.

D.C.?

WASHINGTON, D.C.?

IS THERE ANOTHER D.C.? THIS GUY!

YEAH, I IMAGINE.

OH, I'VE, UH, I'VE NEVER LEFT THE TERRITORIES BEFORE.

WHY THE FUCK WOULD YA? NOTHIN' OUT THERE.

SO, I, UH...

WHAT DO I DO EXACTLY?

YOU'LL TAKE THE TRAIN DOWN TA D.C., YOU'LL STAY AT THE AMBASSADOR FOR THE NIGHT, DELIVER THIS TO OUR GUY AND YOU'LL COME HOME TOMORROW.

I'M LEAVING TONIGHT?

YEAH.

YOU DON'T WANT ME TO DRIVE?

I CAN DRIVE.

YOU'LL TAKE THE TRAIN DOWN TA D.C., YOU'LL STAY AT THE AMBASSADOR FOR THE NIGHT, DELIVER THIS TO OUR GUY AND YOU'LL COME HOME TOMORROW.

OK.

THIS IS YOUR—LET'S CALL IT A PER DIEM.

WHO AM I MEETING?

SENATOR IDIS FULLER.

A SENATOR?

IS HE EXPECTING ME?

NO.

BUT THE ASSHOLE *SHOULD* BE.

HE'LL HAVE A LOT OF QUESTIONS.

BUT HE'LL OPEN THE CASE AND THEN HE WON'T HAVE ANY MORE QUESTIONS.

*HE* OPENS IT, NOT YOU.

DO, I, UH, GET A RECEIPT?

"WE'RE IN *THEIR* NATION'S CAPITAL."

STRIKE OUT?

COULDN'T FIND HER. WHO IS *SHE?*

SAYS SHE WENT TO SCHOOL WITH MY SISTER.

*SHE—* OH DAMN. SHE DID.

HEY *BRACES.*

YOU— HEY, OH OK. YOU LOOK MUCH BETTER.

I KNOW. *THANK* YOU.

THAT'S A FUNNY ONE.

AN ORAL HISTORY AND NO ONE IS SAYIN' NOTHIN'.

THAT'S EXACTLY WHAT HE SAID?

I'M PARAPHRASING, BUT YEAH.

DID HE CLOSE THE CASE IN FRONT OF YOU?

I DON'T— I DON'T KNOW.

IT'S IMPORTANT.

WHY?

BECAUSE WE'RE TRYING TO DETERMINE IF IT WAS THE BRIEFCASE THAT DID THE JOB.

OF *COURSE* IT WAS.

VALENTINE, LISTEN TO ME... WE WOULDN'T DO THAT TO YOU.

WHY NOT?

RIGHT ON TIME.

JIMMY, YOU REALLY GONNA ACT LIKE THIS AIN'T NO BIG DEAL?

IT AIN'T.

THE HELL'S THE MATTER WITH YOU?

WE'VE DONE THIS SHIT FIFTY TIMES.

YOU REALLY DON'T THINK THIS IS DIFFERENT?

NO.

IT IS WHAT IT IS.

ONE GUY FUCKED UP.

ANOTHER GUY PAYS US TO TAKE CARE OF SAID FUCKUP.

THE END.

MY APOLOGIES TO BOTH OF YOU TWO.

DON BONAVESE.

THEY SAID YOU LEFT THE COUNTRY.

I HAD. ON HOLIDAY. A SCHEDULED TRIP UNRELATED TO YOU OR THIS MESS.

I CAME BACK BECAUSE I KNOW MY ABSENCE MUST HAVE CAUSED BOTH OF YOU A GREAT DEAL OF SUSPICION AND DOUBT.

POOR VALENTINE, YOU'VE BEEN A MADE GUY ALL OF TWO DAYS AND THIS IS WHAT YOU GET.

BUT WE HAD TO BE SURE YOU TWO WERE CLEAN.

I THINK YOU CAN UNDERSTAND THIS FROM MY POINT OF VIEW.

I WANT TO DEAL WITH THIS PERSONALLY, AS A MAN, BUT THIS IS SUDDENLY A VERY DANGEROUS AND UNPLEASANT SITUATION.

GET DRESSED.

THIS WASHINGTON, D.C., INCIDENT COULD CAUSE A WAR BETWEEN THE FAMILIES.

AND WHO KNOWS WHAT THE FEDS WILL TRY BECAUSE OF IT.

AND I DIDN'T WANT EITHER OF YOU TO HAVE ANY DOUBT... I DID NOT SEND YOU TO WASHINGTON TO KILL. I SENT YOU WITH A MESSAGE OF INTIMIDATION.

NOTHING MORE.

JAGGER HAS BEEN RUNNING SUCH ERRANDS FOR ME FOR YEARS.

SHE KNOWS.

I HAVE NO PROBLEM GIVING KILL ORDERS MYSELF.

CHICAGO
YEARS AGO

CRAZY SON OF A BITCH.

NOT TO OVERSTEP MYSELF, MR. GIANCANA.

BUT IF YOU WANT US TO GO BACK DOWN THERE AND TAKE CARE OF THIS RUBY FELLA...

NO NEED, JIMMY.

THIS WILL TAKE CARE OF ITSELF.

HE JUST UP AND WENT AND DID THAT?

AS IT HAS BEEN EXPLAINED TO ME: HE FELT HE OWED US A MARKER. HE FEELS THIS CLEARS IT.

DOES IT?

NO.

JACK RUBY IS AN ASSHOLE. INSANE.

HIS WHOLE FUCKING FAMILY IS INSANE.

YOU BOYS, YOU DID WELL.

I'M SENDING YOU OUT OF THE COUNTRY FOR A FEW MONTHS.

TILL EVERYTHING DIES DOWN.

I HEARD YOU WERE PICKED UP BY DALLAS PD.

GGKK!!

VALENTINE.

SQUEAK

DOMINIC JACKSON
Oh yes.

The days where you old fucks got together and whacked each other.

MICHAEL SANGIACOMO
We'd get together and build what you are sitting on, you piece of shit.

DON CREA
This is a closed-circuit system. No one can see or hear us but us.

MICHAEL SANGIACOMO
Says you.

DON BONAVESE
I am hoping to quickly clear the air among us and if any of you know why and how this happened...

CARMINE GIGANTE
You think it was one of us??!!

DON BONAVESE
It wasn't me or my people but it was someone.

MICHAEL SANGIACOMO
Maybe the guy you sent fucked it in a top hat. Heard it was a kid.

DON BONAVESE
I promise you... I'm looking at it from all angles.

DOMINIC JACKSON
Wasn't my guys. I can tell you that.

CARMINE GIGANTE
I don't send my guys out of my territory and this is exactly fucking why.

DON CREA
You're going to have Feds up your ass, Bonavese. You gave them an excuse.

MICHAEL SANGIACOMO
They're going to be up all our asses and it's on you as far as I'm concerned.

DON BONAVESE
I was hoping to keep this civil.

MICHAEL SANGIACOMO
And I was hoping you wouldn't put us in this fucking position.

DOMINIC JACKSON
Yo, man, it wasn't him that did this. He said it wasn't him- it wasn't him. We have to take each other on each other's word.

MICHAEL SANGIACOMO
If he'd leave our ways well the fuck alone and stay to his part of the beach, he wouldn't have no reason to be sending his guys to Washington in the first fucking place. This is how we lost Cleveland.

DON CREA
Again, with fucking Cleveland.

MICHAEL SANGIACOMO
Yes. Yes, again with fucking Cleveland.

Those who don't know their history and all that shit...

Do you know the amount of money we left on the table when we gave up Cleveland??!!

DOMINIC JACKSON
It's Cleveland... so, I'm guessing over two hundred dollars.

CARMINE GIGANTE
Don Bonavese wants to hear it from us and I want him to hear it from me... it wasn't us.

DON BONAVESE
Thank you, Don Gigante.

MICHAEL SANGIACOMO
Of course, if any of you fucked a donkey this bad, the fuck you'd tell any of us.

CARMINE GIGANTE
True.

MICHAEL SANGIACOMO
And if you fucked it on purpose then-

CARMINE GIGANTE
You'd be able to tell. I have a terrible poker face.

DOMINIC JACKSON
Anyone else think Sangiacomo is being extra fucking rude today? Why don't you calm your old ass down and keep it civil

MICHAEL SANGIACOMO
Fuck me then. I guess I'm- I'm old school. That means you don't whack United Stated senators and you don't talk about whacking United Stated senators on a fucking TV. You want to talk to me? You come fucking see me.

DOMINIC JACKSON
Yeah, let's all fly out to Vegas and listen to father time rip us a new one.

DON CREA
You're taking care of this, I assume, Don Bonavese?

DON BONAVESE
Of course. I just want to keep everything aboveboard among us.

DOMINIC JACKSON
You'll keep us posted on all this...

DON BONAVESE
And if any of you hear anything...

CARMINE GIGANTE
You know, the old man was right about one thing...

DON BONAVESE
What's that, Carmine?

CHINK

AGH...

FUCK...

CHINK

MMFFR...

ARE YOU FUCKING KIDDING ME?

THANK YOU FOR NOT KILLING ME AND GOING ABOUT THIS ALONE.

YOU COULD HAVE.

FIRST OF ALL, YOU'RE A MADE GUY.

BUT THE REASON I WAS- THE REASON THE DON ASKED ME TO FOLLOW YOU TO WASHINGTON IN THE FIRST PLACE IS BECAUSE THEY THINK OF ME AS SOMEONE WHO PROTECTS THEIR INTERESTS.

WELL, I'M STILL ALIVE BECAUSE OF YOU SO YOU DIDN'T SCREW IT ALL UP.

BUT THOSE CIA HITGUYS- YOU DID *KILL* SOME OF THEM.

THEY'RE JUST GOING TO SEND MORE.

I LET YOU DOWN.

I LET THE FAMILY DOWN.

I SHOULD HAVE BEEN SIX STEPS AHEAD OF THIS-

ALL I DID MY ENTIRE CHILDHOOD WAS TRAIN FOR THIS AND- AND I SCREWED IT ALL UP.

YOU BETTER BELIEVE IT.

THAT'S WHY WE'RE HERE INSTEAD OF THERE.

I'M READY TO FIND THE FUCKERS WHO DID THIS TO US.

GOOD.

I DON'T HAVE ANY MONEY.

I HAVE MONEY.

YOU KNOW WHAT?

I KNOW HOW TO FIX THIS.

VALENTINE?

VALENTINE, IT'S YOUR MOTHER...

CALL ME WHEN YOU GET UP, OR COME OVER. WE CAN FIGURE THIS OUT.

I LOVE YOU.

KNOCK KNOCK

VALENTINE...

AND SO I TOLD THESE GUYS, YOU SELL NOW YOU'LL BE LOOKING AT NOTHING BUT YOUR DICK IN YOUR—

UH, WARREN, I THINK YOUR NEXT APPOINTMENT IS HERE.

NO CAMERAS IN HERE.

AT LEAST THERE BETTER NOT BE. THIS IS MY PLACE.

YOU'RE NOT MADE AND THEY GAVE YOU A CASINO APARTMENT IN THE FAMILY TOWER? WOW.

WHO DID YOU HAVE TO BLOW?

JUST ABOUT EVERYONE.

DELILAH, IF YOU HEARD ABOUT DINO DOES THAT MEAN YOU HEARD WHAT HAPPENED TO US?

YOU KILLED ONE OF THEIR SENATORS.

WE *DIDN'T*, ACTUALLY.

THEN I THINK YOU SHOULD TELL SOMEBODY BECAUSE A LOT OF PEOPLE THINK YOU DID.

INCLUDING TWO OF THEIR SENATORS WHO ARE STAYING HERE THIS WEEKEND.

WE'RE IN TROUBLE. THE C.I.A. IS AFTER US.

IF YOU CAN FUCKING BELIEVE THAT.

WELL I WISH YOU WOULD'VE TOLD ME THAT BEFORE I BROUGHT YOU UP TO MY HOME.

I THINK MAYBE YOU SHOULDN'T TELL ANYBODY ELSE THAT BY THE WAY.

I AGREE. KEEP IT TO YOURSELF.

AND MAYBE GET THE HELL OUT OF NEW YORK.

WE NEED TO FIND OUT WHO DID THIS, CLEAR OUR NAMES, AND SHUT THIS DOWN.

HAVE YOU HEARD ANYTHING ABOUT ANYTHING THAT COULD POINT US IN THE RIGHT DIRECTION?

THIP

WHAT THE FUCK DID YOU JUST DO?!!!

I TOLD YOU.

I TOLD YOU COMING HERE WAS A FUCKING MISTAKE!

SHE- SHE WAS MY FRIEND.

SHE JUST FED YOU TO THE GOLANNO LIONS, YOU DUMB ASSHOLE.

YOU KILLED MY FRIEND!!!

SHE WAS MY FRIEND.

ARE YOU FUCKING KIDDING ME WITH THIS?

AND YOU KNOW WHAT? FUCK YOU.

I SAVED YOUR FUCKING LIFE AND THIS IS HOW YOU-

CREEAK

THROUGH THE KITCHEN.

SMART ASS.

HEY!

BITCH!!

YOU JUST KILLED MY BROTHER!!

YEAH, WELL, HE SHOT FIRST.

WHO AM I TALKING TO? ANYONE I KNOW?

YOU'RE NOT TALKING YOUR WAY OUT OF THIS ONE, ROSE.

I DO KNOW YOU.

CHICAGO. THE ELECTION COMMITTEE FUCK-UP.

SANCHEZ.

FUCK.

BAD?

HE'S NUTS. I MEAN...

WHO'S HE WORK FOR?

GOLANNO FAMILY.

WELL, THAT ANSWERS THAT QUESTION.

TRUE.

WHY IS THE GOLANNO FAMILY TRYING TO KILL US FOR KILLING A SENATOR WE DIDN'T KILL?

I'LL ASK HIM. HEY, SANCHEZ!!

FUCK YOU, CUNT.

WHY'D YOUR BOSS PUT THE HIT OUT ON US?

MADONNA GALLO.

WHERE AM I?

MY NAME IS HACKMAN.

WE'VE NEVER MET BUT I'VE BEEN WORKING ALONGSIDE YOUR CASE FOR A LONG TIME.

YOU'RE FBI?

I AM.

I AM GOING TO EXPLAIN WHERE I'M COMING FROM...

YOU SEE, YEARS AGO WHEN YOU CAME TO THE FBI AND YOU TOLD THEM OF YOUR PLAN AND YOUR MOTIVATIONS FOR RAISING YOUR CHILD AS A COVERT DOUBLE-AGENT INSIDE THE FAMILY FOR US...

I DON'T THINK YOU'LL FIND IT A SURPRISE TO LEARN THAT THERE WERE SKEPTICS AMONG US, AMONG MY COLLEAGUES...

AMONG THE GENERATION OF AGENTS BEFORE US.

WHEN I INHERITED YOUR CASE, I WAS NOT ONE OF THEM.

AND HERE'S WHY...

YOU SEE WE HAVE SOME THINGS IN COMMON, YOU AND I.

YOU GREW UP UNDER THE GENERATIONAL UMBRELLA OF THE BONAVESE FAMILY.

I GREW UP IN A HOUSEHOLD OF LAW ENFORCEMENT.

I AM FIFTH-GENERATION LAW ENFORCEMENT.

LIKE YOU, I WAS TOLD OF A TIME WHEN THINGS WERE DIFFERENT.

WHERE THERE WAS LAW AND ORDER ACROSS THE ENTIRE NATION.

TIMES BEFORE THIS GOVERNMENT BUCKLED TO THE POWER OF THE FIVE FAMILIES.

I KNOW THAT THE WAY THINGS ARE... ARE NOT THE WAY THINGS SHOULD BE.

BUT YOU AND I, WE ARE IN THE MINORITY.

PEOPLE- MOST PEOPLE- JUST WANT THE WAY THINGS ARE TO BE THE WAY THINGS ARE.

MOST PEOPLE JUST WANT TO BE LEFT ALONE WITH THEIR THINGS.

MOST PEOPLE IN THIS WORLD ARE HAPPY THAT THE EAST COAST AND CHICAGO AND VEGAS ARE PLACES WHERE YOU CAN GO AND DO JUST ABOUT ANYTHING TO ANYONE AS LONG AS YOU'RE WILLING TO PAY FOR IT.

HALF THIS COUNTRY IS AN AMUSEMENT PARK FOR FREAKS.

SO I BELIEVE IN THE IDEA THAT THE ONLY WAY TO STOP THIS IS FOR SOMEONE TO BE ON THE INSIDE.

AND THE ONLY WAY TO MAKE THAT HAPPEN IS FOR THEM TO BE BORN AND RAISED.

AND YOU OFFERED UP YOUR SON.

I BELIEVED IN THE IDEA.

BUT YOU FUCKING BLEW IT.

WHAT ARE YOU GOING TO DO TO ME?

GO FUCK YOURSELF.

NO BACKUP PLAN?

THE PLAN WAS YOU TAKE A SIP OF THE DRINK...

OH, THAT'S RIGHT.

SO THIS IS THE BACK-UP PLAN.

YOUR BACK-UP PLAN NEEDS A BACKUP PLAN.

BECAUSE, AND PAY ATTENTION HERE, IT MAY BE THAT I AM IN THE SHITHOUSE WITH THE FAMILIES, BUT IF YOU ASSHOLES ARE CAUGHT IN HERE?

IF YOU SO MUCH AS FORGET TO PUT A *COASTER* DOWN? IF YOU'RE CAUGHT IN *OUR* WORLD?

WHAT I DID TO YOUR "FRIENDS" BACK IN BROOKLYN... THAT WAS *NOTHING.*

ANSWER ME THIS...

NEW JERSEY AIRFIELD, ONE WEEK LATER

# ISSION

TO BE CONTINUED...
IN BOOK 2:
THE UNITED STATES
VS MURDER INC

# THE UNITED STATES OF
# MURDER INC.
# COVER GALLERY

#3

BENDIS!

MACK

MACK

## THE UNITED STATES OF MURDER INC.

### Issue #1 - Script and Sketches
### by Brian Michael Bendis and Michael Avon Oeming

## PAGE 1-

*1- Int. Party room/ backstage- night*

*Our hero, Valentine, is looking right at us with a quizzical look as a woman off-panel adjusts the tie on his very nice suit.*

#### VALENTINE

Mom.

*2- Over Valentine's shoulder, we see his mother, Madonna, almost tearing up, with glassy eyes. Not tears but very emotional eyes.*

*She has these huge eyes and these killer dimples. A woman who still keeps herself together. You can tell that back in the day she was quite something.*

*You can also tell from her big eyes that she has seen a lot of pain and death. A lot of things that have changed her. A lot of secrets that she keeps inside.*

*Even from her son. Her son being the thing in her life she is most proud of.*

#### MADONNA

Shut up.

#### VALENTINE

Are you gonna cry?

#### MADONNA

You wanna slap?

*3- She adjusts the lapel on his suit. She is so proud of him. All dimples. She holds it together. He looks down at her and can't help but be amazed. Truly.*

*Behind them, a few silhouettes. Men of means waiting in the wings.*

#### VALENTINE

I've never seen you even come close, Ma.

I'm allowed to declare this an historic event.

#### MADONNA

Shut your fuckin' mouth.

*4- Valentine feels her unconditional love. She knows it's time to let go. The wheels are in motion and there's nothing she can do to stop what's about to happen.*

#### MADONNA (CONT'D)

M'not gonna kiss you because I don't want to get any make up or nothin' on ya.

### VALENTINE

Go sit, ma.

You're freakin' me out.

*5- Valentine watches as his mother walks away into the shadows.*

### OLD MAN (OFFPANEL)

You ready, Mr. Gallo?

*6- Valentine is peeking behind the curtain to the stage. Nothing too obvious just a slab of light giving him a look at his future.*

*Behind Valentine, a rotund old man, Bonavese, with a walking cane. Standing behind him ominously. Think Bob Hoskins.*

### BONAVESE

Valentine, you ready?

### VALENTINE

Am I, Padrino?

### BONAVESE

Follow me.

## PAGE 2-

*1- Large panel. Over Valentine's shoulder, many men armed with guns, in light suits, are standing around a table. In the center of the table there is a human skull sitting on top of a piece of paper and a knife.*

*The shadows are so thick behind this ceremony that we can't tell where we are or who else is in the room.*

*2- Low looking up, Valentine approaches and looks down at...*

*3- Valentine's p.o.v. The human skull sitting on top of the top of a piece of paper and a very ornate knife.*

*On the piece of paper is the image of a saint.*

*4- Bonavese picks up the knife and looks at it.*

### BONAVESE (CONT'D)

In my day, this ceremony went a little differently.

It was done in a backroom. Away from the world.

And you had to earn it with a lifetime of service.

You had to be more than just blood.

You had to prove your worth and loyalty.

*5- Bonavese holds the knife up to Valentine. Showing it to him. Engraved. Old school. Like four-hundred-years-old old school.*

### BONAVESE (CONT'D)

But your father, and his father before him... they were truly honorable men.

In many ways they were the backbone of this organization, this family...

I would make an exception for you, Valentine, even if our ways had never changed.

Take the knife.

*6- Valentine holds the knife.*

### BONAVESE (CONT'D)

Who we are is who you are.

Do you agree?

### VALENTINE

Yes, sir.

### BONAVESE

Show us.


## PAGE 3-

*1- Valentine holds it to his lower lip. He is getting ready to cut himself.*

*2- Valentine jabs the knife into the inside of his lower lip.*

*3- The knife has blood on it.*

4- Profile. Valentine leans forward and the blood from the wound drips/pours onto the skull.

### BONAVESE (CONT'D)

You honor your father and your father's father with
this blood oath to the family.

5- The blood pours down the front of the skull's face.

6- Bonavese takes the knife himself

7- Bonavese cuts Valentine's finger.

8- Bonavese takes Valentine's hand and smears Valentine's finger blood on the image of the saint.

## PAGE 4-5

Double-page spread

1- From behind Bonavese, Valentine looks to the godfather and wipes his bloody lip. Not sure what is going to happen next.

2- Bonavese picks up the bloody image of the saint. Another man hands him a long match already lit.

3- Bonavese lights the image of the saint on fire.

4- The paper is burning quickly as Bonavese hands it to Valentine.

### BONAVESE (CONT'D)

If you betray your family...

Your flesh will burn like this saint.

5- Valentine looks at the burning paper in his hand. The saint is burning.

6- The burning paper is almost gone and about to burn Valentine's fingers.

7- Valentine winces as it clearly hurts. A test of endurance.

8- Valentine opens his fingers and the piece of burning paper float into the air. Embers.

### VALENTINE

Ah!

9- The piece of burning paper disappears as it burns itself out.

10- The piece of paper is gone. Just a tiny swirl of smoke.

11- Bonavese pulls out a small gold pin. A circular pin with a symbol on it. A dagger pointed down.

12- Bonavese puts the pin on Valentine's lapel.

13- Valentine turns to see the boss smiling. The serious part is over.

### BONAVESE

And that's that.

14- All the men are smiling and parting ways... some shaking his bloody hand. Bonavese claps his hands and yells out.

### BONAVESE (CONT'D)

Let's eat!!

15- Valentine takes all the good will from his fellow soldiers. His lip still bleeding. A spotlight on him as he looks out and sees...

## PAGE 6-7

Double-page spread

Wide of the party room.

We now see the entire Bonavese family is there. Hundreds of tables of people of all shapes and sizes. Dozens of good families. Mothers, fathers, wives, husbands, children and grandmothers and grandfathers... cousins.

In the old days, the days before things went differently, this ceremony was done in secret in a secret back room but now that the families are an established part of society this ceremony is done in public, in front of the people, like a bar mitzvah or a wedding.

The ceremony part is over and the catering is about to begin. There will be eating and drinking and dancing.

This was Valentine's ceremony. He is a made man.

2- On the bottom of the spread we see that table number one features his mother, Madonna, clapping, still with glassy eyes but no tears.

Other members of his family that really won't play any part of this story.

Except for another guy his same age. His cousin Dino. Thick, strong, curly haired, multi cultural. We imagine his dad was a made guy and his mother was a hooker who had Dino out of wedlock to many's embarrassment. Good guy, good friend, but he is a point of gossip and pity.

Dino is so happy. Applauding. Yelling. This is the best day of their lives.

### DINO

Oh my god!!

Fuck yeah!!

### MADONNA

Be quiet, Dino.

This is CRAZY!!

He did so good!!

---

## PAGE 8-

*1- Ext. Hoboken New Jersey*

*2- Ext. Street*

*3- Ext. Pier c park*

*The Bonavese family headquarters is actually built on the pier C park structure. Instead of being a park it is a family business compound.*

*Instead of the compound being hidden away it is what anyone would see as the real estate crown jewel of New Jersey.*

*This subtle difference shows the family business is done out in the open in opulence. It says everything about what's different about our world.*

*This isn't a sci-fi flying car alternate reality. This is basically our reality with the subtle differences that the mob is doing things out in the open- everything from timeless rituals to how and where they live.*

*A stunning mansion is built on this pier. A small fleet of yachts.*

*4- From behind a man's hand holding a tomato a drink that may or may not have alcohol in it... Valentine is walking across the pier to the opening of the guarded gate.*

*It is not guarded like a mob compound but like the way the White House is guarded.*

*Valentine looks good.*

*5- From behind Valentine, Myer Bloom, a handsome Jewish mob lawyer is enjoying his drink and coming up to shake Valentine's hand.*

### MYER BLOOM

Mr. Gallo.

### VALENTINE

Mr. Bloom.

### MYER BLOOM

First time at the pier?

### VALENTINE

Yes sir.

### MYER BLOOM

Hell of a party last night.

### VALENTINE

Thank you for that.

Really.

*6- They shake hands. All this is new to Valentine. This is his first meeting this high up the food chain.*

*He doesn't know what to expect and everyone's friendly face and politeness is blowing his mind.*

### MYER BLOOM

Don't thank me.

I just do what the big guy says.

How did the rest of your night go?

## PAGE 9-

*1- Int. Hotel room- night*

*Flashback! Valentine is riding the hell out of a busty hooker while another is behind him. We imagine she is shoving her pinky, or something else, right up his ass.*

*The room is trashed. a champagne bottle is open on the bed and soaking the sheet as the three ride each other feverishly.*

*He is shocked at the experience. This is not everyday.*

*2- Ext. Pier c park*

*Resume! Valentine and Myer and walking towards us.*

### VALENTINE

All right.

### MYER BLOOM

You can thank him for that too.

He's waiting for you.

*3- Valentine is escorted through a lovely, well kept garden. Bonavese is in a cobblestone garden. A couple of garden style fancy tables and chairs. The place is perfect.*

*Bonavese is being served tea by a gorgeous Korean woman.*

*Another sharp dressed but relaxed older man, fit, is greeting Valentine. His name is Tony Tuzzo. The underboss.*

### TONY TUZZO

Valentine.

### VALENTINE

Mr. Tuzzo.

*4- Valentine sits at a small table with Tony. My. Bonavese is sipping his tea at another table with a tablet and a newspaper and his tea.*

### TONY TUZZO

So, you ready to get down to it?

### VALENTINE

'Course.

### TONY TUZZO

You understand you won't be working the poker games in town anymore.

### VALENTINE

I actually DIDN'T know that.

### TONY TUZZO

You're a made guy now.

You don't need to be wipin' college shitheads' asses anymore.

You're eventually gonna have people doin' that for you.

#### VALENTINE

So, uh, what WILL I be doing?

*5- Tony looks over to Bonavese, Bonavese doesn't even look at them.*

#### BONAVESE

Tell him.

*6- Over Valentine's shoulder, Tony pulls out a square metal suitcase, small and oddly shaped, and puts it on the table.*

#### TONY TUZZO

Today you're going on a little trip. As a representative of OURS.

#### VALENTINE

Oh.

#### TONY TUZZO

You're gonna go to D.C. and deliver this to a guy.

*7- Valentine is shocked because...*

#### VALENTINE

D.C.?

Washington, D.C.?

## PAGE 10-

*1- Tony is laughing at his stupid question. Bonavese isn't even looking at them. He seems to be reading his paper.*

#### TONY TUZZO

Is there another D.C.? This guy!

#### VALENTINE

Oh, I've, uh, I've never left the territories before.

#### TONY TUZZO

Yeah, I imagine.

Why the fuck would ya? Nothin' out there.

#### VALENTINE

So, I, uh...

What do I do exactly?

*2- Tony hands him a cash envelope clearly full of cash.*

### TONY TUZZO

You'll take the train down ta D.C., you'll stay at the Ambassador for the night, deliver this to our guy and you'll come home tomorrow.

### VALENTINE

I'm leaving tonight?

### TONY TUZZO

Yeah.

### VALENTINE

You don't want me to drive?

I can drive.

*3- Tony is clearly saying that this is the last time you question an order. Handing him a cash envelope.*

### TONY TUZZO

You'll take the train down ta D.C., you'll stay at the Ambassador for the night, deliver this to our guy and you'll come home tomorrow.

### VALENTINE

Ok.

### TONY TUZZO

This is your- let's call it a per diem.

*4- Valentine knows not to count the cash in front of them even though he is clearly dying to.*

### VALENTINE

Who am I meeting?

*5- Tony has a small tablet. Showing him a picture of African-American senator.*

### TONY TUZZO

Senator Idis Fuller.

### VALENTINE

A senator?

Is he expecting me?

6- *Tony gives him a look that says this is more dangerous than you think.*

**TONY TUZZO**

No.

But the asshole SHOULD be.

He'll have a lot of questions.

But he'll open the case and then he won't have any more questions.

HE opens it, not you.

7- *Valentine is stunned by all of this but tries to keep it cool. Not sure if he should ask but...*

**VALENTINE**

Do, I, uh, get a receipt?


# PAGE 11-

1- *Over Valentine's shoulder, Tony belly laughs.*

**TONY TUZZO**

What the fuck are you talking about?

2- *Valentine does not like being laughed at or talked down to. He feels embarrassed in front of the godfather.*

**VALENTINE**

Am I- I don't think these questions are stupid.

I've never done nothin' like this before.

I should walk out of here not knowin' what the fuck I'm doing?

3- *Tony rolls his eyes and calms himself. He sees the kid is pissed even though he doesn't care. No disrespect was meant.*

**TONY TUZZO**

Nah uh. No.

You don't get a receipt.

You come back here you say: package delivered.

4- *Over Tony's shoulder, Valentine is looking over to the Godfather. Not sure if he's taking this too far.*

**VALENTINE**

Can I bring someone?

**TONY TUZZO**

No.

#### VALENTINE

I've- I've never left the territories before. I'd like to
bring someone.

*5- Over Valentine's shoulder, Bonavese finally looks at him. Did Valentine just insult him even though he didn't mean to. Bonavese doesn't take his eyes off the newspaper.*

#### BONAVESE

Your shmuck of a cousin?

#### VALENTINE

He's not a- with all due respect.

#### BONAVESE

His father was a whore-mongering shmuck and
HE is a shmuck.

*6- Over Tony's shoulders, Valentine on the left, and the Godfather on the right, Valentine isn't sure if he should keep this going but...*

#### VALENTINE

I can vouch for him.

#### TONY TUZZO

Jesus!

#### BONAVESE

No you can't.

But you're one of us. It's your call.

And it's on YOUR tab.

I'm not payin' out for that half a whore.

*7- Valentine holds the envelope in one hand and touches the case with the other. Basically downloading all of this information. Making sure he is clear.*

#### VALENTINE

Yes, sir.

*8- Bonavese looks at him for the first time. Completely annoyed.*

#### BONAVESE

Valentine...

Go away.

## PAGE 12-13

*Double-page spread*

*1- Ext. Bullet train to Washington, D.C.*

*Thin panel across both pages.*

### DINO

Fuck me.

*2- Int. Train*

*First-class cabin.*

*Valentine and Dino are taking their seats in the first-class cabin. They sit on the opposite end of the cabin from a handful of slimy young Wall Street assholes that are gathered around the first-class open bar.*

*They are chasing the Asian lady bartender out of the cabin with their obnoxious behavior. They are drunk and coked up and headed to some Georgetown party they think is going to kick ass but probably won't.*

*One guy in particular looks like a young John Tuturo. He is named Eddie.*

*Valentine has the case and is calm and cool. Dino is looking out the window like a puppy. A little under dressed but so excited.*

### WALL STREET ASSHOLE

Oh come on, baby, if I wanted that look I'd'a stayed at home.

### WALL STREET ASSHOLE 2

Good one.

### VALENTINE

Be cool, Dino.

### DINO

We're leavin' the territory. This is crazy!

### VALENTINE

Are you bein' cool?

*2- Two shot. Dino sits in the same couch like seat as Valentine. Looking at him with love. Valentine feels his look and ignores it.*

*3- Same.*

### DINO

You vouched for me.

### VALENTINE

I need a human shield.

AVON 2013

#### DINO

You love me.

*4- Dino and Valentine watch the Wall Street assholes trip over themselves to run the Asian bartender out of the cabin.*

#### WALL STREET ASSHOLE

I mean I want ACTUAL sex on an ACTUAL beach!!

#### WALL STREET ASSHOLE 2

Oh!!

#### VALENTINE

Look at all these Wall Street shmucks. One day to get away from them and there they are.

#### DINO

Hey, fuck 'em.

They pay up just like the rest of us.

#### VALENTINE

Assholes.

*5- Dino and Valentine watch as Eddie is tripping over himself and spilling his drink. Laughing at whatever he just did or said. Spilling a drink.*

#### DINO

For real.

#### VALENTINE

I know that one guy.

#### DINO

Yeah?

#### VALENTINE

What's HE leavin' the territory for?

*6- Dino and Valentine. Dino looks to the left. Valentine staring at the Wall Streeters on the right.*

#### DINO

He's allowed to.

Hey, where'd the redhead from the platform go?

**VALENTINE**

Back in steerage.

*7- Over Dino and Valentine's shoulder, Eddie stand up and drunkenly points at Valentine. Just recognizing him through his drunken haze.*

**EDDIE**

Hey, I know you.

You deal the cards down at you-know-where!

**VALENTINE**

Go siddown, Eddie.

*8- From behind Valentine, Eddie, drunk and stumbling, looks like he is looking for a fight.*

**EDDIE**

The fuck you say to me??

**VALENTINE**

I said go sit down.

Asshole.

*9- Low looking up. Eddie, drunk, about to punch Valentine right in the nose but stops.*

*10- Eddie's p.o.v. The pin.*

*11- Same as nine. Eddie stops himself because he knows what the pin means.*

*12- Valentine looks at him with a cocked eyebrow that says: yeah, go sit the fuck down.*

# PAGE 14-15

*Double-page spread*

*1- Big panel. Dino is up on his feet and clocks Eddie right in the jaw. Hard. No one fucks with his friend.*

    *SPX: WHACK*

*2- 'Camera' on the floor. Eddie hits the floor. His nose blood sprays. Dino is already kicking him.*

    *SPX: FUMP*

**EDDIE**

Oh!

*3- Eddie's p.o.v. Low looking up and wide. Eddie's Wall street friends are stunned. Looking down shocked.*

*4- Same. Eddie's Wall street friends all point and burst out and laugh at him.*

**WALL STREET ASSHOLE**

Aaaaahahahahahaha!!

**WALL STREET ASSHOLE 2**

Douchebag!!

*5- Dino sits down. Valentine is annoyed but at the same time grateful.*

### VALENTINE

He WAS backing off.

### DINO

I already had my arm cocked.

I couldn't stop.

### VALENTINE

And the kick.

### DINO

It's my signature move.

*6- Eddie shaking, crawls to his drunk asshole friends. They laugh at him and throw dollar bills. They make it rain on him.*

### WALL STREET ASSHOLE

Tough guy!!

### WALL STREET ASSHOLE (CONT'D)

Come on, honey, give me a lap dance.

### WALL STREET ASSHOLE 2

That doesn't even make any sense!

*7- Dino and Valentine. Valentine concedes a thank you. Dino, looking off panel to the left, is already deciding to go find the red head.*

### VALENTINE

Thank you.

### DINO

I'm gonna go find the red head.

### VALENTINE

I said thank you.

*8- From over Valentine's head, Dino leaves the car as a woman enters. In the shadows we can just tell a woman is coming in. Pink and purple hair.*

### DINO

Yeah yeah...

*9- Valentine cocks an eyebrow as he sees....*

## PAGE 16-

*1- Page tall. Enter our female lead. Our femme fatale. JAGGER ROSE. She looks amazing. She enters first class and surveys all that she sees. She oozes sex and violence.*

*She owns the room by walking in. Nothing slutty, just smoldering. A practiced perfected move.*

*2- Valentine watches her as Jagger moves over to the bar and the Wall Street idiots. Eddie plugging his nose with tissues as she steps over him.*

*His drunk friends are very taken with her. All eyes on her and she knows it.*

*3- The drunk Wall Streeters watch Jagger slide behind the bar, drop her coat and start making a mixed drink. She looks amazing. Non plussed.*

*4- Eddie drops on the bar and snarls at her.*

### EDDIE

A whiskey.

*5- Jagger continues making her drink. Ignoring him.*

*6- Eddie has had enough shit for one day.*

### EDDIE (CONT'D)

Which part of WHISKEY do you not under-?

## PAGE 17-

*1- From behind Eddie, Jagger takes the bottle she's holding and smashes it over his head. Hard.*

*2- Valentine watches, surprised, as Eddie hits the ground and his friends point in her face to protect him and protest her.*

### WALL STREET ASSHOLE

You DUMB BITCH!!

### WALL STREET ASSHOLE 2

I'm gonna have your JOB, Sally!

*3- Jagger pulls a gun on them. Really nonplussed.*

### JAGGER ROSE

Name's not Sally.

Get off the train.

*4- The Wall Street guys are shocked. Some Laughing.*

### WALL STREET ASSHOLE 2

The fuck you say to-??

*5- Jagger casually SHOOTS HER GUN as she takes a sip of her drink.*

> *SPX: BAM*

# PAGE 18-19

*Double-page spread*

*1- The Wall Streeters freak the fuck out. She grazed one of their arms but she certainly changed the mood of the conversion.*

### WALL STREET ASSHOLE

What the FUCK!??

*2- Jagger is enjoying her drink. Smoking gun up.*

Who's next?

*3- From behind Jagger who pours another drink, gun still up, the Wall Streeters stumble out past Valentine. Eddie on the floor. Out cold and bleeding.*

### WALL STREET ASSHOLE

Fucking goddamn!

### WALL STREET ASSHOLE (CONT'D)

What fucking kind of train?

### WALL STREET ASSHOLE (CONT'D)

Let's just GO!!

I'm bleeding!!

Shot me!!

*4- Valentine calmly watches as Jagger steps over Eddie's body with the two drinks. Heading toward him.*

### VALENTINE

How much are they paying YOU to bartend?

I think I can get you something better in the city...

### JAGGER ROSE

I'm not the bartender, you ass.

*5- Jagger offers him a drink and sits in Dino's seat.*

*Here we get a sense of their chemistry. They are very different from walker and Deena.*

*Although she is a fierce opponent and feisty broad, she is steely eyed and in control, while Deena is wild nervous energy.*

*Valentine is young, a few years younger than her, and very into her. He is trying to be cool but years away from being able to pull it off. But still charming.*

### VALENTINE

Thank you.

Who ARE you?

### JAGGER ROSE

A girl comes onto your train, shows a gun, shoots a guy, and you just sit here?

### VALENTINE

Well, I don't like to judge.

### JAGGER ROSE

No, I'm serious.

How do you know that I'm not here to take the briefcase from you?

*6- He sips his drink. He somehow never considered it but maybe he should have. But he still doesn't think it is an issue.*

*She is sipping her drink and rolling her eyes.*

### VALENTINE

Huh.

Dunno.

### JAGGER ROSE

Sexist.

### VALENTINE

No.

### JAGGER ROSE

If I was a guy-

### VALENTINE

You'd look terrible in that outfit.

*7- She looks at him. Smolder. He puts his foot on the briefcase as to half block it.*

### JAGGER ROSE

You know exactly what I mean.

### VALENTINE

You don't know what's in the briefcase.

### JAGGER ROSE

No.

YOU don't know what's in it.

*8- Same. She sips. He thinks to himself.*

### JAGGER ROSE (CONT'D)

You don't fucking RECOGNIZE me, do you?

### VALENTINE

Um...

### JAGGER ROSE

Really.

### VALENTINE

Did we-?

*9- Flashback! To the sex party last night. He's trying to think if she was one of the call girls. She wasn't. It might be funny to use a stat of the same panel from previously..*

*10- Same as 8. He decides she wasn't there but he's not a hundred per cent. She rolls her eyes to the sky,*

### VALENTINE (CONT'D)

No, that wasn't you...

### JAGGER ROSE

Jesus help me.

*11- Same. Valentine holds out his hand to handshake she doesn't except. Back to sip her drink.*

### VALENTINE

Hi, I'm-

### JAGGER ROSE

Valentine. I KNOW.

I went to school with your sister.

*12- Same. He is stunned. She is subtly annoyed.*

### VALENTINE

We did? You did?

### JAGGER ROSE

Yes. I've slept over your house.

### VALENTINE

Shit, I'm sorry.

You're- um- you're-

*13- Same. She drinks. Muttering to herself.*

### JAGGER ROSE

Jagger- Jagger Rose.

God damn it.

### VALENTINE

Ok.

### JAGGER ROSE

Fuck you.

### VALENTINE

How many colors was your hair back then?

*14- Same.*

### JAGGER ROSE

Put the pin away.

### VALENTINE

What?

### JAGGER ROSE

The coronation pin.

Put it away.

*5- Angle on his made man pin on his lapel.*

## PAGE 20-

*1- Jagger takes the pin and puts it under his lapel. He still wears it but not so anyone can see. He is s little put off.*

### JAGGER ROSE (CONT'D)

We're clearing Baltimore which means that little pin just became an ARREST ME pin.

### VALENTINE

Hey.

### JAGGER ROSE

You are out of the territory and you are out here without a net.

*2- Jagger goes back to her drink. Valentine is genuinely stunned.*

### VALENTINE

Who are you?

### JAGGER ROSE

Don Bonavese sent me.

### VALENTINE

HE sent you?

To do what?

*3- Jagger looks him over. He is trying not to look at her cleavage.*

### JAGGER ROSE

Keep an eye on you.

### VALENTINE

He didn't say anything about you.

### JAGGER ROSE

I know. He finds it funny.

### VALENTINE

You're here to escort me?

*4- Jagger sits back and watches him try not to stare at her boobs.*

### JAGGER ROSE

I'm not an escort.

I'm here to protect you.

### VALENTINE

What?

### JAGGER ROSE

Deal with it.

### VALENTINE

I gotta guy.

### JAGGER ROSE

Yeah? Where is he?

#### VALENTINE

Good point.

*5- From behind Jagger and Valentine, a couple of guys from train security who look just like us comes in and sees the crazy mess.*

#### TRAIN SECURITY

What the-

What the fuck is going on in here?


# PAGE 21-

*1- Jagger pulls out a couple of folded hundreds and smoothly hands it to him.*

#### JAGGER ROSE

Excuse us.

We're on a date.

*2- The security guy takes the cash. His partner eyeballing his half over his shoulder.*

#### TRAIN SECURITY

Yeah, uh, ok.

#### JAGGER ROSE

Thanks.

*3- Jagger leans back and takes a drink. No big deal. He stares at her. In awe now more than any leering.*
*4- Same. She doesn't even look at him.*

#### JAGGER ROSE (CONT'D)

It'll never happen.

#### VALENTINE

What?

#### JAGGER ROSE

I will never sleep with you.

*5- Same. Valentine is uncomfortable. Jagger is a rock. Enjoying her beverage.*

#### VALENTINE

Excuse me.

#### JAGGER ROSE

Your penis will NEVER be in my vagina.

It'll never happen.

### VALENTINE

Yeah, well... Never say never.

### JAGGER ROSE

It'll NEVER happen.

*6- Same. He leans forward. Uncomfortable. Eyeing her out of the side of his eye. Jagger knows it.*

*7- Same.*

### JAGGER ROSE (CONT'D)

Touch my boob.

### VALENTINE

What?

## PAGE 22-

*1- Valentine sits up and looks at her. She has not budged. Sitting back with her drink,*

### JAGGER ROSE

Touch my boob.

All guys think about when they see boobs is how much they want to touch them.

We have work to do.

Touch my boob, right now, demystify them, get it out of your system... and you can focus.

*2- Same.*

### VALENTINE

No.

### JAGGER ROSE

Last chance.

*3- Same. Valentine can't believe her. She sips her drink.*

*4- Same. Valentine thinks about it. He wants to...*

*5- Same. Valentine reaches out and almost touches her boob. She doesn't flinch.*

*6- Same. Valentine decides against it. She doesn't budge.*

### VALENTINE

No.

### JAGGER ROSE

Ok.

Offer rescinded.

We understand each other?

### VALENTINE

You're nuts.

### JAGGER ROSE

Then we understand each other.

Hey look.

## PAGE 23-

*1- Ext. Washington, D.C.*

*The train is pulling into the beautiful Washington, D,C. Iconic.*

*But it is not that opulent. The air is terrible. Sickly. As if something has happened where the air is actually cleaner in the territory than it is in the rest for the world.*

### JAGGER ROSE NARRATION

We're in THEIR nation's capital.

*2- Int. Train station*

*Dino, Val and Jagger are walking through the train station. The Wall street guys are keeping her distance. Others mill about.*

*Tons of uniform angry cops walking around or standing tall. The first cops we have seen.*

### VALENTINE

Strike out?

### DINO

Couldn't find her. Who is SHE?

### VALENTINE

Says she went to school with my sister.

### DINO

SHE- OH DAMN. She did.

Hey BRACES.

*3- Jagger turns around and looks at him as if to say. Do you think that's really how this is going to go. He holds up his hands in surrender. He meant no disrespect.*

### DINO (CONT'D)

You- hey, oh ok. You look much better.

#### JAGGER ROSE

I know.

THANK you.

*4- From behind Val, Val stops at the newsstand and se the one that catches his eyes some books.*

*The book: The United States of Murder Incorporated.*
*How the United States Government Gave up the East Coast to the Mob. By Shecky Finklestien.*

*Other books include: Mice Templar- NOW A MAJOR MOTION PICTURE, Takio the YA novel by Olivia, etc.*

*5- Jagger Rose sees what Valentine is looking at. Dino is staring at one of the cops like he is an alien from outer space.*

#### JAGGER ROSE (CONT'D)

That's a funny one.

An oral history and no one is sayin' nothin'.

## PAGE 24-25

*Double-page spread*

*1- Ext. Washington, D.C./ private club- day*

*A secret club. A member's only club. Something very skull and bones. A type of club for very wealthy and powerful people.*

*2- Ext. Street*

*Across the street, Jagger, Valentine and Dino are watching. Dino still underdressed. Already bored.*

*Behind them a cobble stone half wall and a black spiked fence separating them from a small city park.*

#### JAGGER ROSE (CONT'D)

The Senator is in there.

It's one of those fancy boys only, members only, circle jerks for the elite and powerful.

Don't get any on you.

#### VALENTINE

Let's go.

#### JAGGER ROSE

It's on you.

*3- Valentine looks at Jagger as she gestures to him like a game show hostess. People mill about. The sidewalk is crowded.*

#### JAGGER ROSE (CONT'D)

The Don said this was on you and that is a boys only club.

Put the pin on.

### VALENTINE

You told me to take it off.

*4- Jagger puts it back where she originally unpinned it from. Dino doesn't like her.*

### JAGGER ROSE

And now I'm telling you to put it on.

There are places out here in the wild where you want to wear that pin.

This is one of them.

*5- Int. Club*

*From behind the guard/ host at the opulent dark wood, low light front desk. Valentine walks into the club with the case. Backlit to the front door light.*

### DESK MANAGER

May I help you?

### VALENTINE

I have a package for Senator Fuller.

*6- The man at the desk is about to shoo him away but...*

*7- The desk clerk's p.o.v. He sees the pin.*

*8- The host picks up the phone and at the same time points Valentine down the dark wood many hall full of painting and trophies.*

### DESK MANAGER

Down the hall.

Third room on your right.

The Dupont Club, may I help you?

*9- Doorway- Valentine enters a doorway and looks down at...*

## PAGE 26-

*1- Over Valentine's shoulder, The senator is a very tall African American. 60.*

### VALENTINE

Senator Fuller?

*2- The Senator looks up from his paper with a politician's shit phony smile.*

*3- Small panel. Angle on the pin*

*4- Same as 2. His smiles drops. He knows what this is.*

### SENATOR

How the fuck did you even get in- nevermind.

*5- Valentine hands over that the case. The senator looks at it*

**SENATOR (CONT'D)**

And am I supposed to open this now?

**VALENTINE**

That's completely up to you.

**SENATOR**

I don't understand you people.

*6- Low looking up, fuller is genuinely pissed.*

**SENATOR (CONT'D)**

You have everything you said you wanted.

You have an entire chunk of the country to do that which you may.

And STILL it is not enough.

You're too young to remember what things were like before- this...

THIS is insane.

*7- The senator opens up to the case and looks inside.*

## PAGE 27-

*1- Over the senator's shoulder, it is a foam molded case. Tow compartments. On the left, a beautifully stacked large pile of thousand dollar bills in a perfectly cased foam setting.*

*Right next to it is a dead, bloody bird. Bloody. Also encased.*

*2- The senator looks at him with complete contempt.*

**SENATOR (CONT'D)**

Message received.

Thank you.

*3- Valentine is not sure what he is supposed to do now. Should he leave.*

*4- The senator wants him to leave.*

**SENATOR (CONT'D)**

Is there a singing telegram portion of this message?

No?

Then good-bye.

*5- Ext. Club*

*Valentine walks out of the club into the sunny crowded street.*

*6- Int. Club*

*The senator is so angry. Looking in the case.*

*7- Ext. Street*

*Over Valentine's shoulder, Jagger, across the street eating a street dog, is about to throw it away when...*

*8- Int. Club*

*The senator slams down the case in anger.*

## PAGE 28-29

*Double-page spread*

*Boom. The entire from of the building explodes. The street erupts into chaos.*

*People and cars get hurt. Fire. Blood.*

*Valentine goes flying into a metal gate across the street. He really took a hit.*

## PAGE 30-

*1- Jagger picks herself up. Head ringing. She is scrapped and injured,*

*2- Jagger dives and puts the fire out on a stunned and struggling Valentine's shoulder.*

*3- Valentine looks up. Dazed. Head bleeding. Confused.*

*4- Over Valentine's shoulder, Dino is dead. As are many others.*

*Dino is impaled on the thick black fence that was separating the sidewalk from the small city park.*

*5- Valentine, horrified, dirty, sooty, stares at us. He's in shock. He didn't know what to expect from all of this but he certainly didn't expect any of this.*

## PAGE 31-

*1- Ext. Funeral home/ back room- night*

*Dino lies closed casket. The casket is perspective towards us. At the end of it, Valentine is still in shock. His head bandaged.*

*Clearly they have gotten themselves and Dino out of Washington and back to New York.*

*2- Over Valentine's shoulder, on the other side of this long, cluttered funeral home back room full of coffin parts and wreaths and other things.*

*Jagger is having a heated conversation with Tony and Myer. Clearly something went wrong. Something is wrong. Whatever it is Jagger was not in on it. That is for sure.*

*The mobsters look panicked but are keeping it together. Trying to figure out what happened.*

#### JAGGER ROSE

(muffled) –

Didn't even tell him I was coming and the fucking case was rigged??!!

#### TONY TUZZO

(muffled) – It wasn't!

#### JAGGER ROSE

(muffled)

Are you fucking kidding me!??

*3- Valentine squints. Mistrusting. Blood shot eyes. Unshaven. Did they send him there to die? Did they send him there on a suicide mission without telling him?*

*4- Over Valentine's shoulder, Myer has had enough of Jagger's accusatory shit. Tony is walking up to Valentine with purpose.*

### MYER BLOOM

(muffled)

Enough!! Ok??!! Enough!!

Everyone is fucking upset, goddamn it!!

### TONY TUZZO

I want to hear it from you.

You talked to the guy? The senator?

*5- Tony is right in Valentine's face. Reading his face. Looking for clues of a lie. Valentine is bubbling with rage.*

### VALENTINE

I walked into the club, I handed him the briefcase.

### TONY TUZZO

He opened it in front of you?

### VALENTINE

Yeah.

### TONY TUZZO

You saw what was inside?

### VALENTINE

Yeah.

### TONY TUZZO

What did he say?

*6- Valentine squints. Bloodshot eyes. Unshaven.*

### VALENTINE

He said you were greedy fucking assholes and told me to fuck off.

*7- Valentine's p.o.v. Tony and Myer look at him. Not sure if the insult is coming from him or from the dead senator. Jagger pacing behind them.*

## PAGE 32-

*10 equal size panels. All tight. Suspense.*

*1- Tony is trying to put this together*

### TONY TUZZO

That's exactly what he said?

38

B'GGER?

*2- Valentine is exhausted.*

### VALENTINE

I'm paraphrasing, but yeah.

*3- Same as 1.*

### TONY TUZZO

Did he close the case in front of you?

*4- Same as 2,*

### VALENTINE

I don't- I don't know.

*5- Same as 1,*

### TONY TUZZO

It's important.

*6- Valentine has no idea what he is thinking.*

### VALENTINE

Why?

*7- Tony doesn't understand how valentine doesn't understand...*

### TONY TUZZO

Because we're trying to determine if it was the briefcase that did the job.

*8- Valentine is confused.*

### VALENTINE

Of COURSE it was.

*9- Myer leans in... trying To get this in his head. Sincere. Sweating.*

### MYER BLOOM

Valentine listen to me...

We wouldn't do that to you.

*10- Valentine doesn't know this to be true.*

### VALENTINE

Why not?

## PAGE 33-

*10 equal size panels. All tight. Suspense.*

*1- Same as 9, last page.*

### MYER BLOOM

You're one of us.

*2- Valentine is bubbling with rage.*

### VALENTINE

My friend is DEAD.

*3- Tony points at us. Totayl sincere.*

### TONY TUZZO

Hey, that's on YOU!

We told you not to bring him.

*4- Same as 2.*

### VALENTINE

You're saying YOU didn't do this.

*5- Tony holds up his hand. Sincere.*

### TONY TUZZO

I swear on Christ Almighty.

*6- Same as 4.*

### VALENTINE

I want to hear it from him.

I was to hear it from Don Bonavese.

*7- Myer holds up his hands. There's nothing to discuss.*

### MYER BLOOM

That can't happen at the moment.

*8- Valentine doesn't trust any of this.*

### VALENTINE

Why not?

*9- Same as 7.*

### MYER BLOOM

He's not here.

He left for the old country.

*10- Valentine clearly doesn't believe them*

*Double page spread*

*1- On the other side of the room, Jagger is pacing. She is clearly shaken as well. She may be on Val's side more than he thinks.*

*The men in the background.*

### TONY TUZZO

Maybe you should go home- sleep it off.

### VALENTINE

SLEEP IT OFF?

### TONY TUZZO

Don't worry about your boy.

We'll take care of the arrangements.

*2- Over Valentine's shoulder, Myer sees Valentine doesn't believe them and understands.*

### MYER BLOOM

This is bad business, Val. This is not what we do.

We don't send our soldiers on suicide missions.

We'd HAVE no soldiers.

You see that, right?

*3- Valentine sees the logic but... Val's phone rings.*

### SPX: GLEE GLEE

*4- Valentine looks at his iphone. It's his mom. The mobsters argue behind him.*

*Reads: mom*

### TONY TUZZO

Someone got to the case.

### MYER BLOOM

It wasn't THE CASE!!

### TONY TUZZO

It wasn't the case?? The case just happens to be-

*5- Valentine puts a finger to his ear and turns away from them and answers.*

### VALENTINE

Hello? Ma.

Ma, I'm ok.

What? No.

No reason.

6- *Valentine is walking away from the gangsters as he talks to his mom. Finger to his ear. Annoyed.*

### VALENTINE (CONT'D)

No. I'm ok.

Right now?

Maybe now ain't a good time, Ma.

No, I'm just tired- yeah, I can be there in 20 minutes.

Yeah, yeah, ok...

7- *Valentine, without breaking his stride, hangs up and keeps walking towards us and away from the mobsters.*

### VALENTINE (CONT'D)

I gotta go.

### TONY TUZZO

Best you not say nothin' to no one till we know what the score is.

### MYER BLOOM

We'll get to the bottom of this, Valentine.

We always do.

### TONY TUZZO

We always do.

8- *Valentine is most of the silhouette foreground. Walking away from them. All we can see past him is Jagger hugging herself.*

## PAGE 36-37

*Double-page spread*

*1- Ext. Brooklyn street*

*Valentine, lost in dark thought and despair, walks through the streets of Brooklyn. Colorful and alive. These people feel protected. These people are very used to a very specific way of life.*

*The families have protected this area for so long that they don't know any other way of life.*

*2- Valentine comes to the steps of his mother's nice brownstone. She's dressed smart and already at the door atop the small staircase.*

### MADONNA

What the hell happened to your head?

*3- Valentine has climbed the steps. She is looking at his bandage and isn't happy.*

### VALENTINE

Nothin'.

#### MADONNA

My ass.

#### VALENTINE

It's nothing.

#### MADONNA

A made guy three days and already someone bashed your fucking head in.

#### VALENTINE

Ma.

#### MADONNA

Get in here.

*4- Int. Mom's brownstone*

*Inside her very average, very well kept apartment. Not exactly an old-school Italian apartment... something more modern.*

*A classy, smart, modern woman who has had the place herself for a while. She is doing something nice with it. We imagine that Valentine has made sure that she hasn't ever needed money.*

*She is walking him towards us.*

#### VALENTINE

What was so important?

#### MADONNA

I want you to keep an open mind.

I want you to keep your mouth shut.

#### VALENTINE

What?

#### MADONNA

I'm serious.

I will never be more serious.

*5- Int. Basement steps*

*They are walking into the basement. Bending not to bang his head. One single lightbulb behind them.*

#### VALENTINE

You want me to move something?

*6- Madonna goes to the back wall of typical, cluttered basement shelves. She is reaching into them.*

7- Valentine squints. What is this?

8- Madonna has grabbed the hidden clasp on the back wall.

9- She pulls the clasp and reveals that the shelf wall is actually a door that opens. It reveals itself to be a door.

10- A door to another room that Valentine, although he's lived here his entire life, did not know was there

### VALENTINE (CONT'D)

Since when is this a door?

I lived in this house eighteen years...

### MADONNA

It was your father's panic room.

A safe room. In case something happened.

11- Before they go inside, the light coming from inside the mystery room, she turns around and says to him.

### VALENTINE

Ma, you're freakin' me out.

### MADONNA

I would never put you in this position if I didn't think you were ready.

And I meant what I said: listen. Don't talk.

Do you trust me?

12- Same but tighter. He has no idea what is going on. She wants his full attention.

### VALENTINE

What- the- fuck, Ma?

### MADONNA

Don't make me slap those terrible words out of your mouth.

### VALENTINE

Seriously, what is going on?

13- Over Valentine's shoulder she gives him one last look as she is about to open the door.

## PAGE 38-

1- Big panel. She opens the door and a handsome man and woman in cheap suits with coffee are just standing to great him. Clearly they are FBI. Their names are AGENT GLASS AND AGENT BELL.

It is a very well-lit, clean, white room. With a table and a couple of chairs. And some coffee. That is it.

In the corner we can see there is a monitor that may have been hooked up to some kind of panic room system that has long been outdated.

#### AGENT GLASS

Valentine Gallo, it is a pleasure to meet you.

*2- Valentine cautiously enters the room at his mother's gesture as she closes the door. There was something very odd and alien about this white, well lit, clean room*

#### VALENTINE

The fuck is this?

Do you live in this room?

#### AGENT GLASS

This is a place where we can talk and be sure that no one is listening.

#### VALENTINE

Who would be listening in our kitchen?

*3- Valentine looks at his mom and can't for the life of him figure out what this is about. She is trying to keep him calm but with a mother's stern strong demeanor.*

#### MADONNA

Did I say just sit down and listen?

I said to sit down and listen!

#### VALENTINE

I'll sit down when you tell me what the hell this is.

*4- Over Valentine's shoulder, the agents both know that what they are saying are words that have never been spoken aloud. And once they are said out loud... they can never be taken back.*

#### AGENT GLASS

We're federal agents, Mr. Gallo.

#### AGENT BELL

From outside the territories.

#### AGENT GLASS

Obviously.

*5- Valentine looks at his mother like she is announcing she is an alien from outer space.*

#### MADONNA

And so am I.

*1- That agents lean in and don't give him a second to digest that whopper.*

### AGENT BELL

The families have had their run of things on the east coast for so many years...

I'm not sure you even know there was a time when what they do was considered illegal.

*2- Valentine steps back without even realizing he's doing it as the agents and his mother talk amongst themselves. His back is almost to the closed door.*

### MADONNA

He's not stupid.

### AGENT BELL

It's just people his age-

### MADONNA

How old are YOU?

This is the way it's been since before ALL OF US was born... shut the fuck up.

### VALENTINE

Ma?

*3- Over Valentine's shoulder, his mother sits down and we can feel like a huge weight is being lifted off of her as she says these words she has been dying to say to him for so many years.*

### MADONNA

This isn't how it's supposed to be, Val.

Ok?

The families, the territories...

They- it ain't right.

### VALENTINE

It's- it's the way it is.

### MADONNA

But that don't make it right.

*4- Valentine is appropriately frustrated.*

### VALENTINE

What the fuck are you talking about??!!

You just went to my ceremony!! I'm sworn in by blood!!

*5- Madonna looks right at him and says her ultimate truth.*

#### MADONNA

And you were BORN an undercover federal agent.

*6- Slightly low looking up, Valentine knows that his mother is not joking.*

## PAGE 40

*1- Over Valentine's shoulder, she is looking right at him and telling him how it is.*

#### MADONNA (CONT'D)

I birthed you into this world for this purpose.

No outsider could ever infiltrate the families.

It had to be blood.

It had to be one of us.

*2- Same but tighter. She explains it as clearly as she can.*

#### MADONNA (CONT'D)

They killed your father and your father's father.

They killed them, Val.

No one pays. No one goes to jail.

They just get richer and richer.

So I BIRTHED you into this.

*3- Valentine is open mouthed shocked. This is fucking real??*

#### MADONNA (CONT'D)

All the while praying that this day would never need to come.

That somehow the world would right itself.

But that day never came.

And here we are.

*4- Madonna looks at him and says it with complete confidence*

#### MADONNA (CONT'D)

You're going to pull this all apart, Val.

All of it.

Every single brick. From the inside.

And they'll never even see it coming.

*5- The agents are very excited but trying to keep their composure.*

### AGENT BELL

Do you know what the families did to take control
of this part of the country?

### AGENT GLASS

Does he know who his great-grandfather was?

*6- Madonna stops talking. She looks right at her son. She means business. But this secret will floor him.*

### MADONNA

No.

*7- Valentine looks back at her. He is scared to ask??*


## PAGE 41-

*Full-page spread*

*Ext. The East Coast- sunset*

*The sun sets across the eastern seaboard.*

*The sun sets across The United States of Murder Incorporated.*

*Small white typewriter text across the middle of the spread reads: The United States of Murder Incorporated.*


## TO BE CONTINUED